PHOTOGRAPHIC MEMORIES

Francis Frith's
TORBAY

John Bainbridge

FRITH
BOOK Co

First published in the United Kingdom in 1999 by
Frith Book Company Ltd

Hardback Edition 1999
ISBN 1-85937-063-2

Paperback Edition 2002
ISBN 1-85937-597-9

Reprinted in hardback 2002

British Library Cataloguing in Publication Data

Francis Frith's Around Torbay
John Bainbridge

Frith Book Company Ltd
Frith's Barn, Teffont,
Salisbury, Wiltshire SP3 5QP
Tel: +44 (0) 1722 716 376
Email: info@francisfrith.co.uk
www.francisfrith.co.uk

Printed and bound in Great Britain

As with any historical database the Frith archive is constantly being corrected and improved and the publishers would welcome information on omissions or inaccuracies

Contents

FRANCIS FRITH: *Victorian Pioneer*

FRANCIS FRITH, Victorian founder of the world-famous photographic archive, was a complex and multitudinous man. A devout Quaker and a highly successful Victorian businessman, he was both philosophic by nature and pioneering in outlook.

By 1855 Francis Frith had already established a wholesale grocery business in Liverpool, and sold it for the astonishing sum of £200,000, which is the equivalent today of over £15,000,000. Now a multi-millionaire, he was able to indulge his passion for travel. As a child he had pored over travel books written by early explorers, and his fancy and imagination had been stirred by family holidays to the sublime mountain regions of Wales and Scotland. 'What a land of spirit-stirring and enriching scenes and places!' he had written. He was to return to these scenes of grandeur in later years to 'recapture the thousands of vivid and tender memories', but with a different purpose. Now in his thirties, and captivated by the new science of photography, Frith set out on a series of pioneering journeys to the Nile regions that occupied him from 1856 until 1860.

INTRIGUE AND ADVENTURE

He took with him on his travels a specially-designed wicker carriage that acted as both dark-room and sleeping chamber. These far-flung journeys were packed with intrigue and adventure. In his life story, written when he was sixty-three, Frith tells of being held captive by bandits, and of fighting 'an awful midnight battle to the very point of surrender with a deadly pack of hungry, wild dogs'. Sporting flowing Arab costume, Frith arrived at Akaba by camel seventy years before Lawrence, where he encountered 'desert princes and rival sheikhs, blazing with jewel-hilted swords'.

During these extraordinary adventures he was assiduously exploring the desert regions bordering the Nile and patiently recording the antiquities and peoples with his camera. He was the first photographer to venture beyond the sixth cataract. Africa was still the mysterious 'Dark Continent', and Stanley and Livingstone's historic meeting was a decade into the future. The conditions for picture taking confound belief. He laboured for hours in his wicker dark-room in the sweltering heat of the desert, while the volatile chemicals fizzed dangerously in their trays. Often he was forced to work in remote tombs and caves where conditions were cooler. Back in London he exhibited his photographs and was 'rapturously cheered' by members of the Royal Society. His reputation as a photographer was made overnight. An eminent modern historian has likened their impact on the population of the time to that on our own generation of the first photographs taken on the surface of the moon.

Venture of a Life-Time

Characteristically, Frith quickly spotted the opportunity to create a new business as a specialist publisher of photographs. He lived in an era of immense and sometimes violent change. For the poor in the early part of Victoria's reign work was a drudge and the hours long, and people had precious little free time to enjoy themselves.

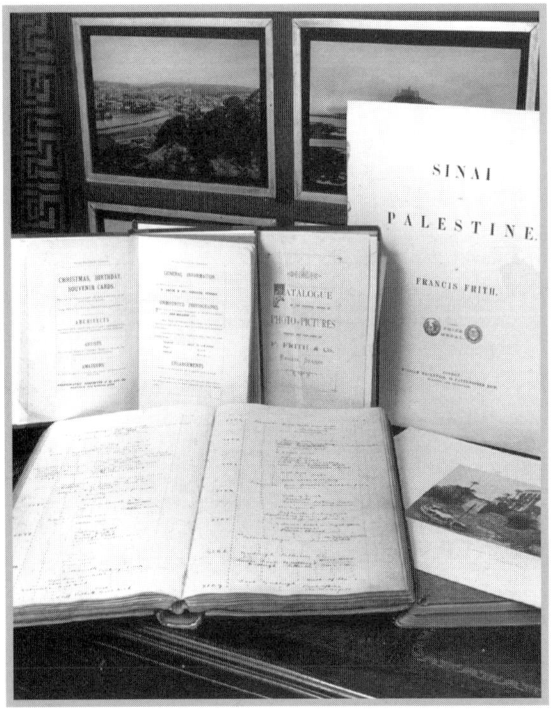

Most had no transport other than a cart or gig at their disposal, and had not travelled far beyond the boundaries of their own town or village. However, by the 1870s, the railways had threaded their way across the country, and Bank Holidays and half-day Saturdays had been made obligatory by Act of Parliament. All of a sudden the ordinary working man and his family were able to enjoy days out and see a little more of the world.

With characteristic business acumen, Francis Frith foresaw that these new tourists would enjoy having souvenirs to commemorate their days out. In 1860 he married Mary Ann Rosling and set out with the intention of photographing every city, town and village in Britain. For the next thirty years he travelled the country by train and by pony and trap, producing fine photographs of seaside resorts and beauty spots that were keenly bought by millions of Victorians. These prints were painstakingly pasted into family albums and pored over during the dark nights of winter, rekindling precious memories of summer excursions.

The Rise of Frith & Co

Frith's studio was soon supplying retail shops all over the country. To meet the demand he gathered about him a small team of photographers, and published the work of independent artist-photographers of the calibre of Roger Fenton and Francis Bedford. In order to gain some understanding of the scale of Frith's business one only has to look at the catalogue issued by Frith & Co in 1886: it runs to some 670

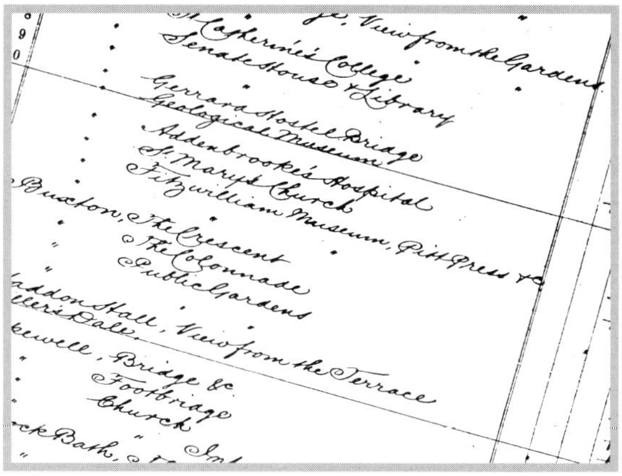
Catherine's College
Senate House & Library
Gerrard Hostel Bridge
Geological Museum
Addenbrooke's Hospital
St Mary's Church
Fitzwilliam Museum, Pitt Press &c
Buxton, The Crescent
The Colonnade
Public Gardens
Haddon Hall, View from the Terrace
Bridge &c
Footbridge
Church

pages, listing not only many thousands of views of the British Isles but also many photographs of most European countries, and China, Japan, the USA and Canada – note the sample page shown above from the hand-written *Frith & Co* ledgers detailing pictures taken. By 1890 Frith had created the greatest specialist photographic publishing company in the world, with over 2,000 outlets – more than the combined number that Boots and WH Smith have today! The picture on the right shows the *Frith & Co* display board at Ingleton in the Yorkshire Dales. Beautifully constructed with mahogany frame and gilt inserts, it could display up to a dozen local scenes.

Postcard Bonanza

The ever-popular holiday postcard we know today took many years to develop. In 1870 the Post Office issued the first plain cards, with a pre-printed stamp on one face. In 1894 they allowed other publishers' cards to be sent through the mail with an attached adhesive halfpenny stamp. Demand grew rapidly, and in 1895 a new size of postcard was permitted called the court card, but there was little room for illustration. In 1899, a year after Frith's death, a new card measuring 5.5 x 3.5 inches became the standard format, but it was not until 1902 that the divided back came into being, with address and message on one face and a full-size illustration on the other. *Frith & Co* were in the vanguard of postcard development, and Frith's sons Eustace and Cyril continued their father's monumental task, expanding the number of views offered to the public and recording more and more places in Britain, as the coasts and countryside were opened up to mass travel.

Francis Frith died in 1898 at his villa in Cannes, his great project still growing. The archive he created continued in business for another seventy years. By 1970 it contained over a third of a million pictures of 7,000 cities, towns and villages. The massive photographic record Frith has left to us stands as a living monument to a special and very remarkable man.

Frith's Archive: *A Unique Legacy*

Francis Frith's legacy to us today is of immense significance and value, for the magnificent archive of evocative photographs he created provides a unique record of change in 7,000 cities, towns and villages throughout Britain over a century and more. Frith and his fellow studio photographers revisited locations many times down the years to update their views, compiling for us an enthralling and colourful pageant of British life and character.

We tend to think of Frith's sepia views of Britain as nostalgic, for most of us use them to conjure up memories of places in our own lives with which we have family associations. It often makes us forget that to Francis Frith they were records of daily life as it was actually being lived in the cities, towns and villages of his day. The Victorian age was one of great and often bewildering change for ordinary people, and though the pictures evoke an impression of slower times, life was as busy and hectic as it is today.

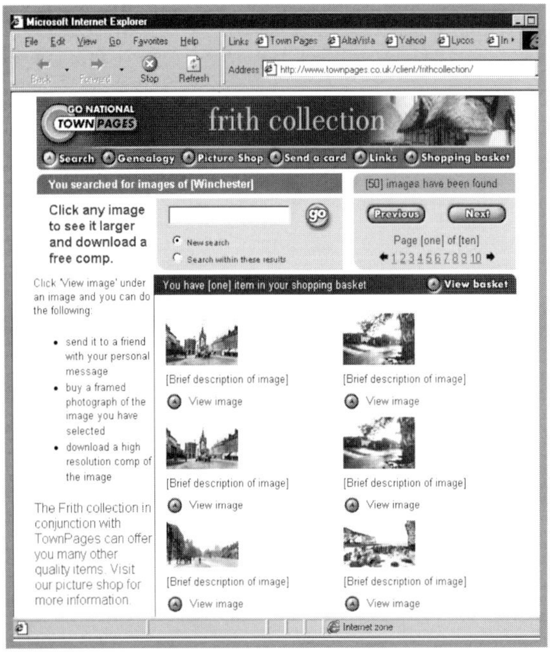

We are fortunate that Frith was a photographer of the people, dedicated to recording the minutiae of everyday life. For it is this sheer wealth of visual data, the painstaking chronicle of changes in dress, transport, street layouts, buildings, housing, engineering and landscape that captivates us so much today. His remarkable images offer us a powerful link with the past and with the lives of our ancestors.

Today's Technology

Computers have now made it possible for Frith's many thousands of images to be accessed almost instantly. In the Frith archive today, each photograph is carefully 'digitised' then stored on a CD Rom. Frith archivists can locate a single photograph amongst thousands within seconds. Views can be catalogued and sorted under a variety of categories of place and content to the immediate benefit of researchers. Inexpensive reference prints can be created for them at the touch of a mouse button, and a wide range of books and other printed materials assembled and published for a wider, more general readership - in the next twelve months over a hundred Frith local history titles will be published! The day-to-day workings of the archive are very different from how they were in Francis Frith's time: imagine the herculean task of sorting through eleven tons of glass negatives as Frith had to do to locate a particular sequence of pictures! Yet the archive still prides itself on maintaining the same high standards of excellence laid down by Francis Frith, including the painstaking cataloguing and indexing of every view.

It is curious to reflect on how the internet now allows researchers in America and elsewhere greater instant access to the archive than Frith himself ever enjoyed. Many thousands of individual views can be called up on screen within seconds on one of the Frith internet sites, enabling people living continents away to revisit the streets of their ancestral home town, or view places in Britain where they have enjoyed holidays. Many overseas researchers welcome the chance to view special theme selections, such as transport, sports, costume and ancient monuments.

We are certain that Francis Frith would have heartily approved of these modern developments, for he himself was always working at the very limits of Victorian photographic technology.

The Value of the Archive Today

Because of the benefits brought by the computer, Frith's images are increasingly studied by social historians, by researchers into genealogy and ancestory, by architects, town planners, and by teachers and schoolchildren involved in local history projects. In addition, the archive offers every one of us a unique opportunity to examine the places where we and our families have lived and worked down the years. Immensely successful in Frith's own era, the archive is now, a century and more on, entering a new phase of popularity.

The Past in Tune with the Future

Historians consider the Francis Frith Collection to be of prime national importance. It is the only archive of its kind remaining in private ownership and has been valued at a million pounds. However, this figure is now rapidly increasing as digital technology enables more and more people around the world to enjoy its benefits.

Francis Frith's archive is now housed in an historic timber barn in the beautiful village of Teffont in Wiltshire. Its founder would not recognize the archive office as it is today. In place of the many thousands of dusty boxes containing glass plate negatives and an all-pervading odour of photographic chemicals, there are now ranks of computer screens. He would be amazed to watch his images travelling round the world at unimaginable speeds through network and internet lines.

The archive's future is both bright and exciting. Francis Frith, with his unshakeable belief in making photographs available to the greatest number of people, would undoubtedly approve of what is being done today with his lifetime's work. His photographs, depicting our shared past, are now bringing pleasure and enlightenment to millions around the world a century and more after his death.

TORBAY – *An Introduction*

TORBAY was famous as an anchorage for naval and merchant vessels long before the first tourists arrived to sample its sandy beaches, warm waters and balmy climate. Sheltered from the notorious south westerly gales that regularly swept up the English Channel, Torbay has been a welcome refuge for shipping from the Middle Ages. In its time, the huge sweep of the bay has been the haunt of Moorish pirates, Elizabethan seadogs and Lord Nelson's navy. In 1815, Napoleon Bonaparte, captured after Waterloo, admired the local scenery, comparing it to Italy and the Isle of Elba, as he paced the decks of HMS Bellerophon on his way to exile. As a strategist, he must also have admired the bay's capability to house the entire British fleet in bad weather. Much of the fleet was at anchor for weeks at a time north of Berry Head, and the first real visitors were the wives and families of naval officers who came to be near to their menfolk. The growth of the Romantic Movement, with its appreciation of wild scenery and love of poets such as Wordsworth and Coleridge, also brought visitors to Torbay.

Yet Torquay, Paignton and Brixham were relative latecomers as holiday resorts. The seaside towns of East Devon and Dorset were already popular by the time the first real tourists arrived in Torbay at the end of the 18th century. The Napoleonic Wars, which kept wealthy travellers away from the continent, boosted Torbay's fortunes.

These first visitors looked upon the kind weather and peaceful ambience of the area as a valuable restorative for their health. In an age when illness could devastate large swathes of the population, the clean air and fresh breezes of the Torbay coastline and the surrounding countryside were a welcome relief from the increasingly industrial towns and cities.

The Frith photographs captured the towns of Torbay at vital times in their development. We see the growth of the holiday trade and the way it progresses, against the background of communities that originated in fishing and farming. In many ways, Torbay has changed more in the past twenty years than in the hundred years which are recorded in these photographs. The family seaside holiday has become a part of social history; today, Britons travel abroad more, and feel less inclined to linger on England's beaches.

Traditional summer and winter residents, for these towns were often as popular for winter breaks as summer ones, have been largely replaced by short-term holidaymakers and day trippers. Many of the fine villas and hotels have been converted into holiday flats or old folk's homes, and the countryside which once gave towns like Paignton and Torquay their discrete identities has been developed and built upon. Only Brixham, isolated behind wild cliffs, fields and woodland, seems to have preserved its personality.

These careful photographic studies by the Frith photographers are, in a way, an epitaph for a vanished world. Yet, as we stroll through the narrow streets, busy promenades and picturesque harbours of Torbay, its echo remains.

TORQUAY – *The Queen of the English Riviera*

TORQUAY sprawls across the northern end of Torbay, the heart of the town lying above and beyond the long golden beaches of Livermead, Corbyn Bay and Abbey Sands. At its eastern borders the scenery becomes wild and romantic, with isolated deepwater coves and rugged grey cliffs curving out into the English Channel. Dense woodland invades even the suburbs, breaking up the urban landscape that now stretches out towards the neighbouring towns of Babbacombe and St Marychurch.

Though a late starter as a holiday resort, Torquay soon acquired popularity with Victorian visitors who came to savour its Mediterranean-like setting and mild climate. Within a few years they had dubbed the growing community 'The Queen of Watering Places', and hurriedly occupied the new villas and luxury hotels that were to double the size of Torquay almost every decade. Even today, when the towns of Torbay comprise the third largest urban area in Devon, Torquay is redeemed by the splendour of its setting and rejoices in its newer designation as 'The Queen of the English Riviera'.

For most of those early years, Torquay catered for invalids, particularly consumptives, who came for the refreshing breezes and quiet relaxation. A Victorian commentator noted that 'the general effect of the white houses, the grey limestone cliffs, and the foliage and greensward forming the ground of the whole, is unusually pleasant and picturesque, calculated to soothe, as far as scenery can soothe, the lassitude and depression of ill-health'.

This combination of nature at its best and some of the stateliest accommodation in Britain has given Torquay a popularity that will probably never entirely fade. But scratch beneath the surface, and it is still possible to identify the villages that were so mercilessly engulfed to form one of the greatest of all seaside towns. Tor Muhon, Torre, St Marychurch, and Cockington; all were important parishes in England's history, but are now overwhelmed by the new town that has either laid siege to, or absorbed them entirely.

Centuries ago the church controlled

much of this landscape from its nearby base of Torre Abbey. By the time of the Dissolution of the Monasteries, Torre Abbey was one of the richest clerical houses in the country and was acquired by the Ridgeway family, Tudor favourites, who built a grand home nearby. Later residents, the Cary family, sold the abbey and land to the Torbay Corporation in 1930 and it is now an impressive local museum and art gallery. A visit will reveal a great deal of knowledge about the history of Torbay, and the museum has an informative section devoted to the life and work of Torquay's most famous daughter, the crime-writer Agatha Christie.

Travellers hurriedly moving between Torquay and Paignton do not usually appreciate that the long seashore road is relatively new. Until the middle of the last century the holidaymaker would have had to take a circuitous route along distant Devon lanes. This new road, originally a turnpiked toll-road, opened to the dismay of the owner of Torre, Mr Cary, who was hostile to the idea of tourists walking and riding in front of Torre Abbey and spoiling his view. The road effectively opened up the long beach of Abbey Sands for bathers and increased the renown of the town for summer visits.

Roads elsewhere shaped the design of the growing resort. Union Street and Fleet Street, which now enable the pedestrian to walk quickly from the top of the town to the harbour, were built later in the 19th century, enclosing the Flete Brook and sweeping away the slums and fishermen's cottages of earlier times. This long thoroughfare now provides Torquay with its principal shopping malls. Victoria Parade, once the home of the poet Elizabeth Barrett Browning, was rebuilt to give access to the growing number of villas around Vane Hill and Ilsham.

Today's tourists, like their Victorian forebears, still like to linger around the harbour, which gives shelter to about 40 acres of the greater anchorage of Torbay. Early visitors would have watched fishermen busily at work, but their successors regard, perhaps a little enviously, the departure of luxury yachts from the marina or queue for more modest boat trips of their own. High above the harbour is the prominent church of St. John, rebuilt by the fashionable London architect G E Street in the 1860s. Its fussy interior might have seemed too 'high church' for its earlier parishioners, but no one can deny the grandeur of its setting. Its view across the harbour and Torbay is unsurpassed in a townscape of wonderful views, and the building itself is a welcome landmark for returning sailors.

Torquay is still a town to explore on foot, as the Frith family clearly did as they searched the area for their ideal pictures. Walking up the narrow streets, steep flights of steps and winding alleys in the vicinity of the town itself, you come unexpectedly on disused quarries, limeburner's kilns and sudden delightful views across the harbour and the great sweep of Torbay. It is still a photographer's paradise!

TORQUAY

From Waldon Hill 1888 21417

Park Hill, seen here across Torquay harbour from Waldon Hill, became a popular residential area at the beginning of the 19th century, sheltered as it was from easterly gales. On the summit is the tower of Vane Hill Villa, a copy of a building on the shore of Italy's Lake Lugano. Much of the architecture of Torquay was Continental in inspiration.

TORQUAY, WALDON HILL FROM PARK HILL 1888 21427
Looking back in the opposite direction, this view shows Waldon Hill and the Strand. Waldon Hill once served as a rabbit warren to supply food for early residents. By 1888, it had become this impressive townscape of fine villas and family hotels.

TORQUAY, ABBEY CRESCENT 1896 38598
The elegant Abbey Crescent was built in 1858 in anticipation of the opening of the nearby railway station the following year. Its designers considered that this new access to Torquay would popularise this hitherto quiet end of the town.

Torquay, Vane Hill 1896 38593
Above Torquay harbour stands Vane Hill, named after the prominent weather-vane placed there in the early 19th century by Mrs Johnes, a local benefactor who spent a great deal of her own money improving the growing town.

Torquay, The Strand 1906 54015
Apart from a considerable increase in traffic, Torquay's Strand has changed very little since this photograph was taken during Edwardian times. The harbour was at that time the preserve of local fishermen, but today the area is monopolised by pleasure craft and luxury yachts.

TORQUAY
Fleet Street 1906 54027
Running above the course of the Flete Brook, this broad street, now one of Torquay's premier shopping malls, was constructed in 1865 to replace the narrow lane of slums and fishermen's cottages. With Union Street, it provides a grand approach to Torquay Harbour from the top of the town.

TORQUAY, ST. MARY MAGDALENE CHURCH 1912 64688

St. Mary Magdalene Church was designed and built for the people of Torquay by Anthony Salvin, famous for his restoration of Windsor Castle, and built in 1848-9. Its fine spire and simple lines still dominate Union Street and Castle Circus.

Torquay, St. Marychurch 1920 69605

St. Marychurch was one of the original small parishes that made up the new town of Torquay. The church was razed to the ground during an air raid on 30 May 1943, tragically killing 26 children and their teachers. It has now been sympathetically restored.

Torquay, Fishermen 1888 21445

Before the coming of tourism Torquay was an obscure fishing hamlet, its villagers scratching a living from fishing, lime burning and smuggling. All of these activities continued well into the Victorian Age. These fishermen on a Torbay beach carried on their traditional way of life regardless of the spread of hotels and villas.

Torquay

From the Pier 1888 21444

In-shore net fishing was carried out by a combination of men on the beach and small boats at sea. Fishing remained a major industry in Torbay until well into the 20th century, though some fishermen diversified into tourism, offering boat trips to places of interest round the bay.

TORQUAY, FROM ODDICOMBE BEACH 1889 21491
By 1889, the holidaymakers had discovered the spectacular coves around Babbacombe. Oddicombe Beach became a popular venue for walks and swimming, as these bathing machines show. Oscar Wilde and the Prince of Wales, later King Edward VII, were frequent visitors.

TORQUAY, THE ROCK WALK 1901 47811
In the 1850s Torquay was being compared to Montpelier and the South of France, and had been dubbed the 'Queen of Watering Places'. Even by the time this picture of the Rock Walk was taken, Torquay remained a mid-Victorian town in design and atmosphere.

Torquay, Rock Walk 1906 54019
Promenaders seek shade under Torbay's famous palm trees along the Rock Walk. On warm days, the South Devon coast can be as hot and humid as more tropical resorts, and a number of sheltered walks were designed to aid the retention of the fashionable, pale complexion.

TORQUAY

Corbyn Head 1904 52951

The cliffs of Corbyn Head divide the famous Torquay beaches of Torre Abbey Sands and Livermead. With the growth of Paignton in the early 1900s, Livermead became the most popular of the Torbay beaches.

TORQUAY
Corbyn Heart 1920 69593
The spread of bathing huts around the heart-shaped Corbyn Beach indicates the popularity of this far end of Torre Abbey Sands - it offered safe and sheltered swimming and paddling.

TORQUAY, PRINCESS PARADE 1920 69579

In the 1920s Torquay became not only a location for family holidays but also a much-loved venue for day trips, with tourists arriving by train and charabanc. Torquay had been an escape from the horrors of the Great War, and many ex-servicemen returned as they attempted to adjust to peacetime living.

TORQUAY, TORBAY ROAD 1920 69592
Horse-drawn vehicles were giving way to motor traffic in the early 1920s, as this fine study of Torbay Road shows. The open-top omnibuses plied their trade between Torquay and Paignton, halting at all the popular beaches along the way.

TORQUAY
Abbey Sands 1924 76401
On a crowded summer's day, sunbathers enjoy the warmth on Abbey Sands. Modesty dictated that bathers should get into their costumes in one of the long line of changing tents.

TICKET OFFICE.

TORQUAY, ABBEY SANDS PARK 1924 76397

TORQUAY

Abbey Sands Park 1924

As Torquay developed into a resort for people of all backgrounds, so a range of activities was provided for days when sea-bathing was impossible. Here the tourists play games, promenade or just sit and reflect as they gaze down on Abbey Sands.

TORQUAY

Grand Hotel 1924

With the decline in the building of villas, large and impressive hotels were built to cater for richer visitors arriving at the nearby railway station. The Grand Hotel was frequented by many famous celebrities such as Noel Coward and Agatha Christie, who was born not far away and spent her honeymoon here.

TORQUAY, GRAND HOTEL 1924 76414

Torquay, Oddicombe Beach 1924 76428

Before the development of Babbacombe as a holiday resort, the isolated coves on either side of Torbay were well used by smugglers such as Bob Elliott of Brixham and Jack Rattenbury of Beer. The present coastal footpath came into being as a regular patrol route for coastguards charged with preventing the landing of illicit cargo.

TORQUAY, ODDICOMBE BEACH 1924 76431
When this picture was taken, visitors to Oddicombe Beach faced a steep climb up and down from the town of Babbacombe, situated high on the top of the cliff. Two years later the famous cliff railway, still in use today, was opened, making the journey very much easier.

TORQUAY, TORBAY ROAD 1924 76403
On a bright summer day hordes of tourists enjoy all that is best about a seaside holiday in Torquay. The First World War had closed the Continent to visitors and Devon resorts had come into their own again, retaining their popularity in the harsh 1920s when money was in short supply.

TORQUAY, TORBAY ROAD 1928 81116

Torbay Road was constructed in 1840 as a turnpike providing the first direct link between Torquay and Paignton. At the time Mr Cary, the owner of nearby Torre Abbey, had objected to the intrusion of the new route in front of his home. He argued that the proposed road would be vulnerable to the sea. He was right: Torbay Road often has to be closed during winter easterly gales.

TORQUAY, TORBAY ROAD 1924 76408

Torquay in the twenties was renowned as a refined holiday resort. By 1930, Torre Abbey and its parklands, on the left in this picture, had been acquired by the Borough Council for the use of residents and visitors.

TORQUAY

St. John's Church and the Harbour 1890 25921

St. John's Church, situated dramatically above Torquay Harbour, was built in limestone excavated from its own site in 1861. The architect was G E Street. The west window was designed by the Pre-Raphaelite painter Edward Burne-Jones.

VAULTS

TORQUAY, THE HARBOUR 1924 76411
Beyond Torquay Harbour is the fine sweep of Torbay, with the sheltering arm of Berry Head in the distance safeguarding this famous anchorage. By the 1920s the whole of Torbay had become popular for leisure boating, but the more commercial shipping trade had begun to decline.

TORQUAY, THE HARBOUR 1928 81106
For many years Torquay Harbour was used for commercial merchant shipping as well as for fishing and pleasure craft. 'Tip and Run' air raids in the Second World War led to the decline in this use of the harbour. With the construction of the harbour marina, Torquay became a popular mooring for the owners of luxury yachts.

PAIGNTON – *The Town of Golden Sands*

PAIGNTON'S role as the family resort of Torbay began relatively late in the town's history. Two hundred years ago the place was hardly more than a village, dependent on farming and fishing for the livelihood of its inhabitants. Their way of life could scarcely have changed very much since Paignton was recorded as Peintone in the Domesday Book of 1086. The original Saxon village had probably existed for three centuries before that, named Paegintun, Paega's Farmstead, the summer home of the bishops of Exeter.

Even when the first tourists began to arrive, the traditional industries continued; cider and cabbages were shipped in great quantities to London until the end of the 19th century. Although never a fishing port on the scale of Brixham, boats regularly put to sea from the small harbour constructed under Roundham Head, half a mile from the main village. A causeway across the marshy ground was built to facilitate the journey from homestead to harbour. Its site runs along the line of the present Sands Road.

The old Saxon street layout can still be seen near St. John's church. The original building was replaced by the Normans in about 1100 and remained important in ecclesiastical history, thanks to the patronage of Exeter's bishops. The Palace of the See of Exeter remained intact until Tudor times and a few remnants survive today. Miles Coverdale occupied the Palace in the mid-16th century and is said to have produced his famous translation of the Bible there. While historians cast some doubt on the probability of that tradition, the old Palace tower in the vicarage garden is still called the 'Bible Tower' in commemoration of the event.

In the forty years that followed the opening of Paignton railway station in 1859, the population of Paignton trebled, as hotels and villas were hurriedly built to cope with the massive influx of tourists. As a holiday resort Paignton pitched for the middle ground, neither seeking the exclusivity of Torquay or the quaintness of Brixham. Almost from the start it sought out the newly affluent families of middle England, who actually wanted to just paddle and swim along the two miles of safe beaches, or promenade along the pier or sea wall on balmy evenings, rather than mix with high society or improve their minds.

The whole geography of Paignton was transformed to cater for the taste of these temporary residents. The huge marsh, which had once divided the village from the sea, was drained and contained behind the wide stone-built promenade, its old heartland becoming the pleasure ground of Paignton Green. Hotels and villas rapidly ate up the green distance between parish church and strand. As if this was not enough, the townsfolk, determined to provide enough attractions to stop visitors wandering off to the neighbouring resorts, laid out the patriotically-named Queen's Park and Victoria Park, followed soon afterwards by Palace Avenue Gardens.

There was little danger, however, of Paignton going too down-market. Isaac Singer, the sewing machine millionaire, chose Paignton over the more refined Torquay as the setting. There was little danger, however, of Paignton going too down-market. Isaac Singer, the sewing machine millionaire, chose Paignton over the more refined Torquay as the setting for his imposing new mansion at Oldway, which he had built in 1874 at the then extravagant cost of £100,000. The great building, inspired by the Palace of Versailles, was not completed until 1907, under the guidance of Isaac's son Paris Singer. Paris Singer brought most of London society down to Paignton, including his lover, the dancer Isadora Duncan.

Since the early days, many tourists have decided to settle in and around the town, and this residential population probably kept local services going as the holidaymakers fled abroad in search of the sun. But Paignton reinvented itself as a destination for short breaks and touring holidays. Holiday camps around the bay provided alternative breaks and aided the prosperity of the town. Winter holidays are again becoming fashionable for the visitor who wishes to seek out the delights of Devon at a less crowded time of the year. Paignton has come a long way since it was a simple Saxon homestead, but its long story goes on.

PAIGNTON, VICTORIA STREET 1912 64718

Paignton was recorded in the Domesday Book of 1086 as Peintone, Paega's farmstead, and was a Saxon colony long before that. Even before the Norman Conquest the tiny village became the property of the Bishops of Exeter, who built a summer palace nearby.

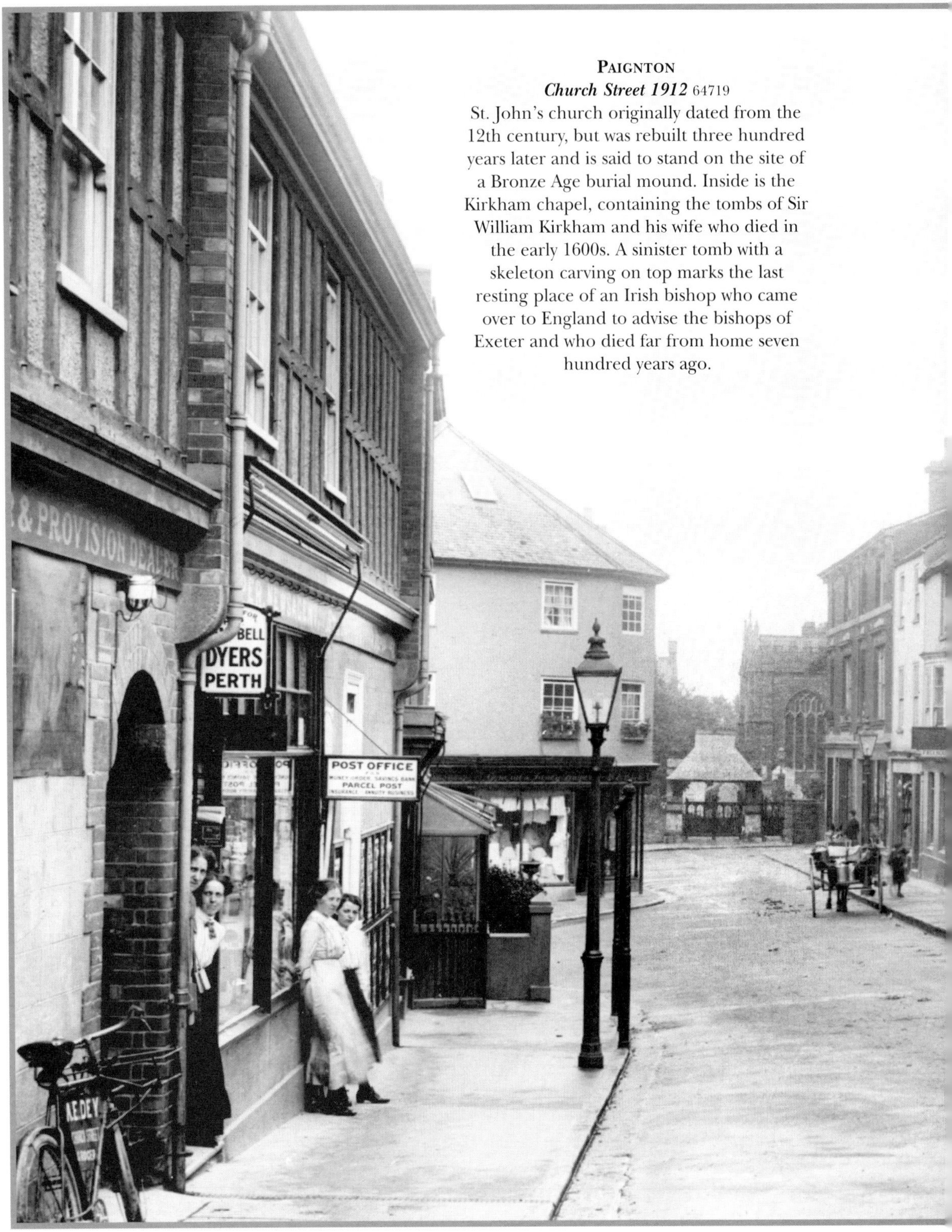

PAIGNTON

Church Street 1912 64719

St. John's church originally dated from the 12th century, but was rebuilt three hundred years later and is said to stand on the site of a Bronze Age burial mound. Inside is the Kirkham chapel, containing the tombs of Sir William Kirkham and his wife who died in the early 1600s. A sinister tomb with a skeleton carving on top marks the last resting place of an Irish bishop who came over to England to advise the bishops of Exeter and who died far from home seven hundred years ago.

POOK BROS
FAMILY BUTCHERS
MACDONALD
POOK BROS

PAIGNTON

Gerston Hotel 1907 58429

Paignton's safe bathing beaches led to the construction of a great many family hotels; so much so that the inland town near to the church was spreading towards the sea by mid-Victorian times, to cope with the massive influx of summer visitors. To the rear of the Gerston hotel was the tiny Royal Bijou Theatre, where Gilbert and Sullivan's 'The Pirates of Penzance' was first performed.

GERSTON
HOTEL

PAIGNTON HARBOUR 1890 25907

PAIGNTON HARBOUR
1890

The harbour at Paignton is an extension of a simpler shelter for shipping, which probably existed from the Middle Ages. Though not as sheltered as Brixham Harbour, it maintained a fishing fleet for several centuries. Today it is used mainly for leisure boating.

PAIGNTON HARBOUR FROM ABOVE
1890

Like Brixham, Paignton was a ship building centre, though generally the vessels were smaller than those launched elsewhere. The harbour was often used by merchant coasters, which brought goods into the expanding town until the trade declined with the coming of the railway.

PAIGNTON HARBOUR FROM ABOVE 1890 25906

PAIGNTON HARBOUR 1894 33646
By later Victorian times hotels, pubs and villas had clustered around Paignton Harbour, much as we see them today. However, the harbour itself had declined in importance, except for the occasional coaster and in-shore fishing smacks.

PAIGNTON HARBOUR 1922 73067
By the 1920s, the harbour was used almost entirely by small-scale fishermen and pleasure craft. Here we see the nets and lobster pots of local fishermen, who had begun to diversify into pleasure trips and boat-hire to increase their income.

Paignton Harbour 1922 73068
One famous Paignton sailor was William Adams, who was born in the town in 1612. On a long voyage home his ship was captured by a Turkish privateer and he was kept as a slave in Algiers for five years before managing to escape and return home. He lived to have many more adventures before dying at home in 1687, where he is buried in the churchyard.

The Pier, Paignton 1889 21529
Paignton pier, one of the oldest in Britain, strides 800 feet out to sea and is seen here in all its finery. Only Paignton has a pier of all the Torbay towns, probably owing to a combination of its popularity as a family resort and the gently sloping sands that facilitated its construction.

Paignton, The Pier and Sands from the Esplanade 1896 38560
The growth of leisure in the 1890s led to the rapid growth of seaside towns like Paignton, which could be used as touring centres as well as holiday resorts. Cycling had become a popular and cheap way to explore the countryside for both sexes.

PAIGNTON, THE PIER AND NORTH SANDS 38549
From the earliest days of leisure, a stroll along the pier became an essential part of a summer holiday. Paignton's pier was used both for promenading and to access the pleasure boats that would ply their trade of trips around the bay and fishing excursions.

PAIGNTON
North Sands from the Pier 1896
The Paignton beaches and coves give a combined sea-frontage of over two miles, and this led to the growth of the town's satellite villages of Goodrington and Preston. These long stretches of sand offer the safest bathing of all the Torbay resorts.

PAIGNTON
The Club House and Esplanade 1896
Paignton Club House overlooked the Esplanade and sea front, and was the favoured meeting place of 'the better class of visitor' until the Great War. It was considered by the residents of neighbouring Torquay that even the 'better classes' who stayed in Paignton might not be quite 'top drawer'.

PAIGNTON, NORTH SANDS FROM THE PIER 1896 38550

PAIGNTON, THE CLUB HOUSE AND ESPLANADE 1896 38555

PAIGNTON

The Esplanade 1896 38558

Paignton became fashionable with the arrival of the Singer family, who built the imposing Oldway Mansion in 1874. The sewing machine millionaires completed their home in 1907, inspired by the architectural wonders of Versailles. The cream of Victorian society visited the Singers at their imposing seaside home.

Paignton

The Bathing Beach 1896 38545

Sea bathing was a much-enjoyed activity in which most people who could afford a holiday indulged. Queen Victoria regularly held forth on its benefits for 'the constitution' of her subjects and often participated herself. Both sexes bathed together at Paignton, though bathing machines were used to preserve a sense of decorum.

PAIGNTON, THE PROMENADE AND SANDS 1907 58415a
This view shows the inhabitants of an England at peace with itself and confident of its position in the world. The long 'Edwardian Afternoon' had only a few more years to run before the death of the king and the first shots of a world war.

PAIGNTON
The Sea Front 1912
Paignton Green, though originally marshy ground and frequently invaded by high tides, was speedily turned into a pleasure ground after the building of the sea wall and promenade. By this time, motor vehicles were becoming a regular sight in the Torbay towns.

PAIGNTON
The Esplanade 1912
A timeless scene, early in the reign of King George V; ladies and gentlemen, heavily suited for a summer holiday, with a governess for the children, lazily admire the scenery, while a cyclist wheels her bicycle wearily along the Promenade.

PAIGNTON, THE SEA FRONT 1912 64711

PAIGNTON, THE ESPLANADE 1912 64713

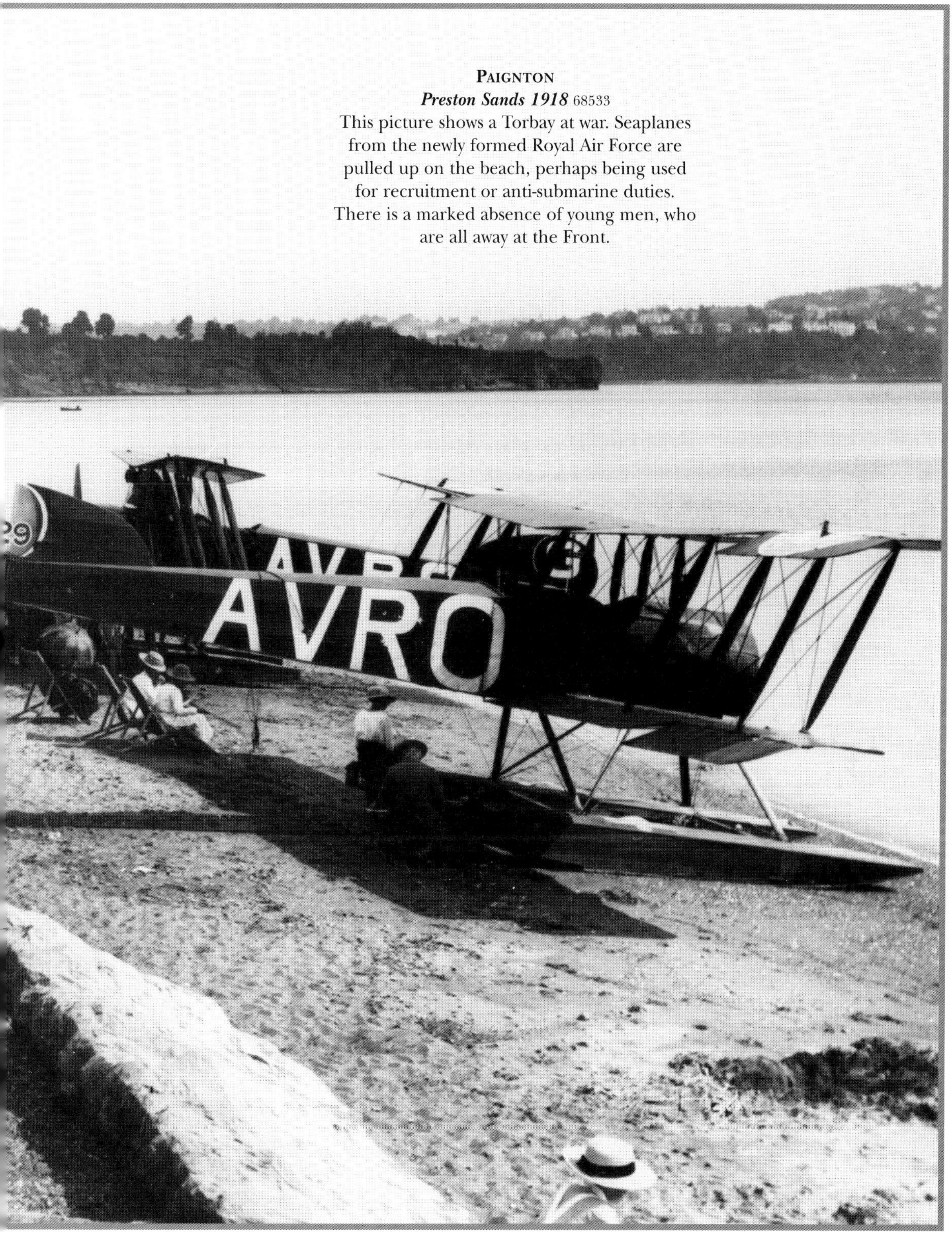

PAIGNTON
Preston Sands 1918 68533
This picture shows a Torbay at war. Seaplanes from the newly formed Royal Air Force are pulled up on the beach, perhaps being used for recruitment or anti-submarine duties. There is a marked absence of young men, who are all away at the Front.

PAIGNTON, PRESTON SANDS 1922 73071
Preston lies at the north end of the Paignton sea front. By the 1920s its long sands were challenging the popularity of both Torquay and Paignton itself. The increase in population led to Preston becoming a heavily built-up area, and a great deal of open countryside was lost from this time onwards.

PAIGNTON, THE SANDS 1925 78479
By 1925 Paignton had firmly established its reputation as a family resort. Here a boatman lures tourists with the promise of trips round the bay, while family groups paddle and swim nearby. Most excursions from Paignton went from the beach, rather than the harbour, because that is where most of the tourists could be found. Hence the boarding ramps to enable passengers to walk out to the boats that could not come right up the gently sloping beaches.

PAIGNTON, THE SANDS 1925 78480
The pattern of seaside holidays remained unchanged until well after the Second World War, when affluence meant that more British holidaymakers could travel abroad. Towns like Paignton survived by promoting shorter breaks and publicising the delights of Paignton as a touring centre.

PAIGNTON, DELLER'S SUMMER CAFE 1928 81153A
Deller's summer cafe, one of a famous chain, was a favourite place to visit for traditional cream teas. The service industry sprang up early in the 20th century to serve the increasing number of tourists.

PAIGNTON, THE GREEN 1925 78481
Many of the hotels in the background had started life as luxury villas, but were soon adapted to hotel and boarding house use. Very often several terraced private houses were transformed into single buildings to allow for the flexibility demanded for family holidays.

BRIXHAM – *The Old Town of the Sea*

BRIXHAM hides at the southern end of Torbay, sheltered from the wild channel gales by the dark and towering cliffs of Berry Head. Throughout the town's history, this neighbouring headland has protected its inhabitants from more than the weather. From the Iron Age, Berry Head had been fortified against invasion. Here anxious residents scanned the English Channel far below for Vikings, Moorish privateers and the Spanish Armada. The visitor today, walking out to see the now-automatic lighthouse, will pass through a complex series of Napoleonic forts and will see evidence of defences from the Second World War.

The significance of Torbay as a safe anchorage for naval and merchant vessels cannot be underestimated, nor can the importance of the Brixham fishing industry to the local and national economy. Brixham harbour dates from at least the 11th century and it rapidly overtook Paignton as a fishing port. From the earliest times, the fishermen of Brixham refined the art of trawl-netting as a way of catching fish nearer to the sea floor. In the days of sailing this would have involved going out to sea in severe weather, so that the wind could propel the trawlers fast enough to keep the net moving through the water without folding or snagging. It was a profitable, if hazardous, way to make a living. Many of the boats would have been share-owned by family and friends and in good years the tiny town enjoyed an affluence rarely seen elsewhere. Brixham was, as the novelist and diarist Fanny Burney noted, ' a most excellent fishing town, but very dirty and disreputable'. Compared to the London social scene it probably was, but its good fortune and successful harvesting of the sea gave it a lower death rate per head of population than that of most similar-sized towns in England.

Brixham enjoys its moment in English history. The statue of William of Orange looks away from the harbour towards the London road, much as William himself must have looked, considering his fortunes after a Brixham fisherman carried him ashore on 5 November 1688. He had come, he told the astonished townsfolk, 'to maintain the liberties of England and the Protestant religion'. As befits a maritime port, the fishermen and their families took the accompanying Dutch sailors into their homes and their hearts, before helping the new king on his way to the throne.

Brixham developed rather late as a holiday resort, refusing to compromise its traditional industries of fishing and boat building simply to attract visitors. Few hotels existed, and the absence of long sandy beaches kept traditional holidaymakers away. Those that did arrive would have been put up in local inns or in fishermen's cottages. But the town's attractive setting did appeal to the more romantic and artistic eye, and visitors soon began to arrive from the crowded resorts of Paignton and Torbay.

By Victorian times it is said that the local vicar, the Reverend Henry Francis Lyte, could walk across the harbour on the decks of the anchored fishing fleet, as he preached to his flock before they set out to sea. Henry Lyte loved the town and its inhabitants and was adored in return. He lived for many years high on the cliffs at Berry Head House, walking down to preach at the new church of All Saints, or often on the harbourside itself. In ill health, he penned the words of the hymn 'Abide with Me' not long before being forced by illness into exile in the south of France, where he died of consumption soon afterwards.

Generations of Brixham fishermen have sung Lyte's hymn as they have set out to sea:

Hold Thou Thy Cross before my closing eyes,
Shine through the gloom and point me to the skies;
Heaven's morning breaks and Earth's vain shadows flee;
Help of the helpless, O abide with me.

Lyte's church of All Saints was rebuilt in 1907, with the support of local fishing families, as a memorial to its first and much-loved vicar. A carillon of bells plays Lyte's hymns throughout the day, and 'Abide with Me' echoes over the ancient harbour during the still of evening.

Brixham, General View 1896 38885

Brixham
General View 1896
Despite its fame as a fishing port from the Middle Ages onwards, people have lived around Brixham for some half a million years. Caves under the limestone cliffs were occupied from the early Stone Age. Iron Age dwellers built a fortification on Berry Head and Celtic inhabitants would have collected salt and caught fish where the harbour stands now.

Brixham
The Approaches 1896
Easily approached in most weathers, Brixham Harbour was a natural sanctuary even within the sheltered waters of Torbay. The breakwater is 3000 feet long and protects an area of 140 acres. This peaceful anchorage is as appreciated by yachtsmen as it is by present day fishermen.

Brixham, The Approaches 1896 38889

BRIXHAM

General View 1896 38882

Early in the 19th century, twelve Brixham fishermen used their profits to buy a one-fourth share in the Lordship of the Manor of Brixham. These shares have been divided and sub-divided so much that most Brixham fishermen with a longstanding connection to the old town might rightly be referred to as 'M'lord'.

BRIXHAM, THE FISHING FLEET 1896 38893
Every evening the bells of All Saints Church peal out the tune of Henry Francis Lyte's immortal hymn, 'Abide with Me', over Brixham Harbour. Lyte wrote the hymn when he was already dying of consumption and soon before he had to leave Brixham for good. The hymn achieved great popularity and Brixham fishermen would recite the words as a prayer as they set out to sea.

BRIXHAM, THE HARBOUR 1896 38887
Fishermen's cottages look down on a quiet harbour. Brixham women would knit jerseys, as well as make and repair nets and rope while the fishing fleet was at sea. In stormy weather, when the fleet was overdue, the families of the fishermen would line the walls of the harbour, braving the rains and gales for a first glimpse of the returning fishing boats.

BRIXHAM, THE INNER HARBOUR 1889 21552
After the 1850s, the new railway from Churston meant that Brixham fish could be sent swiftly to towns and cities throughout Britain. Most Brixham trawlers were owned by shareholders, with family, friends and neighbours holding shares. Brixham enjoyed a prosperity rarely seen during the hard times of Victorian England.

BRIXHAM, A SHIP BUILDING YARD 1904 53147
Until the 20th century, shipbuilding was Brixham's most important industry after fishing. Small merchant vessels and privateers were constructed during earlier times for trade and piracy, though in later years many of the shipbuilders concentrated on building and repairing fishing boats.

BRIXHAM, THE FISHING FLEET 1889 21558

BRIXHAM, THE OUTER HARBOUR 1924 76453

BRIXHAM

The Fishing Fleet 1889

This idyllic picture of the Brixham fishing fleet gives some idea of just how much the fishing industry dominated the town for hundreds of years. At the height of the Victorian age, some 200 trawlers would regularly put to sea from Brixham Harbour.

BRIXHAM

The Outer Harbour 1924

Brixham has known sadness and tragedy as well as the tough but idyllic life of its fishing heyday. Two hundred Brixham men died during the First World War, many of them fishermen. This led to a declining fishing industry and an idle fleet during the depression of the 1920s.

BRIXHAM, COTTAGES 1922 73038
In the quiet streets and winding alleys of Brixham, families wait for the fishing fleet to return safely home. During the 1920s fishing in Brixham suffered from the effects of economic depression and the number of boats putting to sea declined. For the first time in decades the town's fisherfolk experienced real poverty. Though the industry recovered, Brixham was never to see again the great fleets setting out to sea.

BRIXHAM

The Harbour with All Saints Church 1925 78489

The Reverend Lyte's church of All Saints stands proudly above the winding streets of the town. Inside is a memorial to the author of 'Praise My Soul, The King of Heaven' and 'Abide With Me'. Visitors in 1925 would probably have been as moved by the tablet to Tom Littler, killed in France a few years earlier, which contains the touching epitaph from Chaucer, 'He loved chivalry, truth and honour, freedom and courtesy; he was a very perfect gentle knight'.

ME 6102
BM 3

Brixham

The Harbour 1925 78490

Fishing boats lie idle in the midst of the recession of the 1920s. Many fishermen went out of business altogether, and others fished only occasionally. Hard-pressed Brixham fishermen found some relief by providing boating trips for the burgeoning family tourist industry, line fishing and trips around the bay.

BRIXHAM, THE HARBOUR 1925 78487
An almost empty harbour during the recession. Long gone were the days when it was possible for locals to cross the harbour on the decks of the fishing fleet at anchor. In these empty years, Brixham became a haunt for those seeking the picturesque. Artists and photographers captured the romance of a lost way of life.

BRIXHAM, STATUE OF WILLIAM OF ORANGE 1925 78492
William of Orange, whose statue looks away from the sea and towards England, landed at Brixham on 5 November 1688 to depose the Catholic King James II and to herald 'a Glorious Revolution'. William and his Dutch troops received a hearty welcome from local families.

Brixham, Fishing Harbour c1955 B214313

The fishermen of Brixham refined the technique of trawling for their catch close to the bottom of the sea, which replaced the earlier technique of drifting. The sailing trawlers needed to work with the tide and had to work with a stiff wind (up to force six or seven) behind them if the nets were to be trawled successfully.

BRIXHAM, THE JETTY 1955 B214107
By the 1950s, a modern diesel fishing fleet had restored Brixham's reputation as an important fishing port. With an increase in tourism the little town began to prosper again. The fishermen themselves became a favourite tourist attraction.

BRIXHAM, THE PARISH CHURCH 1922 73048
St Mary's, the parish church of Higher Brixham, was the original place of worship, dating back to the 15th century. There are some impressive altar tombs inside and a font dating back to the 1300s. This church tends to be missed by visitors, who speed by to see the Rev. Lyte's new church of All Saints, which stands so prominently above the harbour.

Brixham
Berry Head Lighthouse c1955
The bold promontory of Berry Head guards the south western approaches to Torbay. Its prominent position has led to a series of forts being constructed on its high cliffs from the Iron Age to more modern times. The lighthouse building might be tiny, but its height above the sea means that its beam can be seen for many miles.

Brixham
Berry Head House 1925
Constructed as a military hospital during the Napoleonic Wars, Berry Head House's most famous resident was the much-loved Rev. Henry Francis Lyte, who wrote many of his famous hymns while living there. This fine building is now an hotel.

Brixham, Berry Head Lighthouse c1955 B214165

Brixham, Berry Head House 1925 78496

BRIXHAM

Fore Street 1922 73032

For many years Brixham's Fore Street was the principal thoroughfare down to the harbour from Higher Brixham and the rest of Torbay. Here we see it at a time when the shops mostly catered to local fishing families. Notice the horse-drawn cart and the absence of much other traffic.

THE CAFÉ
ALL KODAK SUPPLIES
VELOX

BRIXHAM, FORE STREET 1955 B214077
Here we see the same street in the 1950s. Many of the smaller shops had survived, though the chain stores were beginning to arrive and greater numbers of tourists were discovering the delights of Brixham.

BRIXHAM, FORE STREET 1965 B214318
By the 1960s traffic was starting to clog up Fore Street and the first double-yellow lines had appeared. Many shops were now selling tourist souvenirs rather than purely local produce for local needs. So bad did Brixham's traffic problem become that several streets, including this one, were eventually pedestrianised.

Brixham, Coffin House 1922 73041

Building a community under the rocky cliffs of Brixham led to many unusually-shaped buildings designed to fit into odd corners of the steep and winding streets, as this photograph of the famous Coffin House illustrates.

INDEX

Frith Book Co 1999 Titles

From 2000 we aim at publishing 100 new books each year. For latest catalogue please contact Frith Book Co

Barnstaple	1-85937-084-5	£12.99	Oct 99
Blackpool	1-85937-049-7	£12.99	Sep 99
Bognor Regis	1-85937-055-1	£12.99	Sep 99
Bristol	1-85937-050-0	£12.99	Sep 99
Cambridge	1-85937-092-6	£12.99	Oct 99
Cambridgeshire	1-85937-086-1	£14.99	Nov 99
Cheshire	1-85937-045-4	£14.99	Sep 99
Chester	1-85937-090-X	£12.99	Nov 99
Chesterfield	1-85937-071-3	£12.99	Sep 99
Chichester	1-85937-089-6	£12.99	Nov 99
Cornwall	1-85937-054-3	£14.99	Sep 99
Cotswolds	1-85937-099-3	£14.99	Nov 99

Derby	1-85937-046-2	£12.99	Sep 99
Devon	1-85937-052-7	£14.99	Sep 99
Dorset	1-85937-075-6	£14.99	Oct 99
Dorset Coast	1-85937-062-4	£14.99	Sep 99
Dublin	1-85937-058-6	£12.99	Sep 99
East Anglia	1-85937-059-4	£14.99	Sep 99
Eastbourne	1-85937-061-6	£12.99	Sep 99
English Castles	1-85937-078-0	£14.99	Oct 99
Essex	1-85937-082-9	£14.99	Nov 99
Falmouth	1-85937-066-7	£12.99	Sep 99
Hampshire	1-85937-064-0	£14.99	Sep 99
Hertfordshire	1-85937-079-9	£14.99	Nov 99
Isle of Man	1-85937-065-9	£14.99	Sep 99
Liverpool	1-85937-051-9	£12.99	Sep 99

Maidstone	1-85937-056-X	£12.99	Sep 99
Northumberland & Tyne and Wear	1-85937-072-1	£14.99	Sep 99
North Yorkshire	1-85937-048-9	£14.99	Sep 99
Nottingham	1-85937-060-8	£12.99	Sep 99
Oxfordshire	1-85937-076-4	£14.99	Oct 99
Penzance	1-85937-069-1	£12.99	Sep 99
Reading	1-85937-087-X	£12.99	Nov 99
St Ives	1-85937-068-3	£12.99	Sep 99
Salisbury	1-85937-091-8	£12.99	Nov 99
Scarborough	1-85937-104-3	£12.99	Sep 99
Scottish Castles	1-85937-077-2	£14.99	Oct 99
Sevenoaks and Tonbridge	1-85937-057-8	£12.99	Sep 99
Sheffield and S Yorkshire	1-85937-070-5	£12.99	Sep 99
Shropshire	1-85937-083-7	£14.99	Nov 99
Southampton	1-85937-088-8	£12.99	Nov 99
Staffordshire	1-85937-047-0	£14.99	Sep 99
Stratford upon Avon	1-85937-098-5	£12.99	Nov 99
Suffolk	1-85937-074-8	£14.99	Oct 99
Surrey	1-85937-081-0	£14.99	Oct 99
Torbay	1-85937-063-2	£12.99	Sep 99
Wiltshire	1-85937-053-5	£14.99	Sep 99

British Life A Century Ago

246 x 189mm
144pp, hardback.
Black and white
Lavishly illustrated with photos from the turn of the century, and with extensive commentary. It offers a unique insight into the social history and heritage of bygone Britain.

1-85937-103-5 £17.99 ....

Available from your local bookshop or from the publisher

Frith Products & Services

Francis Frith would doubtless be pleased to know that the pioneering publishing venture he started in 1860 still continues today. More than a hundred and thirty years later, The Francis Frith Collection continues in the same innovative tradition and is now one of the foremost publishers of vintage photographs in the world. Some of the current activities include:

Interior Decoration

Today Frith's photographs can be seen framed and as giant wall murals in thousands of pubs, restaurants, hotels, banks, retail stores and other public buildings throughout the country. In every case they enhance the unique local atmosphere of the places they depict and provide reminders of gentler days in an increasingly busy and frenetic world.

Product Promotions

Frith products have been used by many major companies to promote the sales of their own products or to reinforce their own history and heritage. Brands include Hovis bread, Courage beers, Scots Porage Oats, Colman's mustard, Cadbury's foods, Mellow Birds coffee, Dunhill pipe tobacco, Guinness, and Bulmer's Cider.

Genealogy and Family History

As the interest in family history and roots grows world-wide, more and more people are turning to Frith's photographs of Great Britain for images of the towns, villages and streets where their ancestors lived; and, of course, photographs of the churches and chapels where their ancestors were christened, married and buried are an essential part of every genealogy tree and family album.

A series of easy-to-use CD Roms is planned for publication, and an increasing number of Frith photographs will be able to be viewed on specialist genealogy sites. A growing range of Frith books will be available on CD.

The Internet

Already thousands of Frith photographs can be viewed and purchased on the internet. By the end of the year 2000 some 60,000 Frith photographs will be available on the internet. The number of sites is constantly expanding, each focussing on different products and services from the Collection.

Some of the sites are listed below.

www.townpages.co.uk
www.familystorehouse.com
www.britannia.com
www.icollector.com
www.barclaysquare.co.uk
www.cornwall-online.co.uk

For background information on the Collection look at the two following sites:

www.francisfrith.com
www.francisfrith.co.uk

Frith Products

All Frith photographs are available Framed or just as Mounted Prints, and can be ordered from the address below. From time to time other products - Address Books, Calendars, Table Mats, Postcards etc - are available.

The Frith Collectors' Guild

In response to the many customers who enjoy collecting Frith photographs we have created the Frith Collectors' Guild. Members are entitled to a range of benefits, including a regular magazine, special discounts and special limited edition products.

For further information: if you would like further information on any of the above aspects of the Frith business please contact us at the address below:

The Francis Frith Collection, Frith's Barn, Teffont, Salisbury, Wiltshire England SP3 5QP.
Tel: +44 (0) 1722 716 376 Fax: +44 (0) 1722 716 881 Email: frithbook.co.uk

To receive your FREE Mounted Print

Cut out this Voucher and return it with your remittance for £1.50 to cover postage and handling. Choose any photograph included in this book. Your SEPIA print will be A4 in size, and mounted in a cream mount with burgundy rule lines, overall size 14 x 11 inches.

Order additional Mounted Prints at HALF PRICE (only £7.49 each*)
If there are further pictures you would like to order, possibly as gifts for friends and family, acquire them at half price (no additional postage and handling required).

Have your Mounted Prints framed*
For an additional £14.95 per print you can have your chosen Mounted Print framed in an elegant polished wood and gilt moulding, overall size 16 x 13 inches (no additional postage and handling required).

*** IMPORTANT!**
These special prices are only available if ordered using the original voucher on this page (no copies permitted) and at the same time as your free Mounted Print, for delivery to the same address

Voucher for FREE and Reduced Price Frith Prints

Picture no.	Page number	Qty	Mounted @ £7.49	Framed + £14.95	Total Cost
		1	**Free of charge***	£	£
			£	£	£
			£	£	£
			£	£	£
			£	£	£
			£	£	£
				* Post & handling	£1.50
				Total Order Cost	**£**

Title: TORBAY

063-2

Please do not photocopy this voucher. Only the original is valid, so please cut it out and return it to us.

I enclose a cheque / postal order for £ . . . .
made payable to 'The Francis Frith Collection'
OR please debit my Mastercard / Visa / Switch / Amex card

Number . . . .

Expires . . . . Signature . . . .

Name Mr/Mrs/Ms ....

Address ....

....

....

....

.... Postcode ....

Daytime Tel No .... Valid to 31/12/01

Frith Collectors' Guild

From time to time we publish a magazine of news and stories about Frith photographs and further special offers of Frith products. If you would like 12 months FREE membership, please return this form and we will send you a New Member Pack.

Send completed forms to:
The Francis Frith Collection, Frith's Barn, Teffont, Salisbury, Wiltshire SP3 5QP

The Francis Frith Collectors' Guild

I would like to receive the New Members Pack offering 12 months FREE membership.

063-2

Name Mr/Mrs/Ms ....

Address ....

....

....

.... Postcode ....